NEW WINE

A Journey into refueling your life in the spirit

Dr. Susan Agbenoto

ISBN 979-8-89043-051-9 (paperback)
ISBN 979-8-89043-052-6 (digital)

Copyright © 2024 by Dr. Susan Agbenoto

All rights reserved. No part of this publication may be reproduced, distributed, or transmitted in any form or by any means, including photocopying, recording, or other electronic or mechanical methods without the prior written permission of the publisher. For permission requests, solicit the publisher via the address below.

Christian Faith Publishing
832 Park Avenue
Meadville, PA 16335
www.christianfaithpublishing.com

Printed in the United States of America

To my Lord and Savior Jesus Christ.

To my beloved family, who have been my inspiration and my greatest fans.

Foreword

As I move through the chapters of this book, I can only say thank you. What a great message to the people of the church. Apparently, you have put words together that reminds us we need to turn back to God. Dr. Susan Agbenoto you have put a great deal of time and energy in relating our need for a revival. I pray every reader of this work be inspired to have a desire to know God better. Yes, there is a need for a revival. Lord God, please help us repent of our wickedness and commit ourselves totally you and for your Kingdom. Thank you for the history of those who preached fire and truth of repentance through Jesus Christ. As I read this book I pray for the same calling. The pouring out of the Holy Spirit for this last day harvest. I pray for workers, witnesses and those who will invite those who are perishing. I really miss the old time religion, where Spirit of God would rule the hearts of man. Thank you for this work.

Rev. Dr. Drorester Alexander,
Senior Pastor, United Methodist Church.

Preface

There are times when you ask the question, *is this all there is to life?* Or yet, still you experience a certain dryness on the inside, which affects all that you do. Perhaps you need the *new wine* of the Lord to stir you up. This is a compilation of narratives to stir you up deep within your spirit, to provoke you to hunger for more, and not to give up on the promise of greater things ahead.

No matter what you have been through, how you went through it, and even how many years you have seen, there is more ahead for you. The Lord is not done with you. He will, at times, purposely agitate your soul to stir you up to seek him on a different level. When one has been in one place for a while, one tends to think that "everything" is happening there. It is not true. God is a great God doing wondrous things in many different places. Sometimes, like he did with the prophets, he will call you out to a different place to speak to you so you can see what he is doing over there. Usually, you will return with a new perspective, a fresh fire, with the taste of *new wine*. This spurs you on to achieve more, to pursue more, and to fulfill the destiny God has for you with passion and fruitfulness.

As you read through this book, receive a fresh wind of the spirit. May you be provoked to pursue all that God has for you. May you experience personal revival. May you also be used as a vessel of corporate revival.

DR. SUSAN AGBENOTO

May you bear even more fruit and accomplish even greater works. May you experience the *new wine* of the Lord. Your best days are ahead!

Introduction

> Where there is new wine
> There is new power
> There is new freedom
> And the kingdom is here
> I lay down my old flames
> To carry your new fire today
>
> —New Wine, Hillsong Worship[1]

This writing is not about red versus white wine. It is not about whether Italian or California vineyards produce the best-tasting fermented beverages. It is about the spiritual drink that fills you and causes you to bubble up with zeal so that it seems as if you are intoxicated. At different points in scripture, we see the comparison between wine and the effects of being filled with the spirit of God. Some centuries ago, on a day when the disciples of Jesus and others were gathered in one place, there was a great visitation of the Holy Spirit. It is known today as the Day of Pentecost. They describe the sounds as coming from heaven, with the similitude of a rushing mighty wind. Then they describe what they saw as looking like tongues of fire sitting upon every-

---

[1] New Wine (CMG song #202782), Brooke Ligertwood. Used with permission.

one present. The effect of this visitation caused them to exhibit behaviors such as speaking in other tongues, fervent prayers, groaning, joy and laughter, incessant recounting of the events, and so on.

Today, similar visitations are called *revivals*. Some who observed them said, *They are filled with new wine* (Acts 2:13 ESV). Also in the book of Ephesians, we are counseled, *And do not get drunk with wine, for this is debauchery, but be filled with the Spirit* (Ephesians 5:18, ESV). There are similarities in the effects of physical drunkenness and spiritual drunkenness as we see in the behavior of those who experienced the visitation of Pentecost. The difference is the source. One gives life, and the other is an agent of disease and death, according to statistics. Being filled with this new wine of the Lord will satisfy your inner thirst, will dispel the dryness of your spiritual walk, fill you with joy, and will cause you to bubble over with words of exhortations, prophecies, prayers, and songs. It will cause you to be fruitful, even as you desire to be used as a conduit of the move of God. Receiving new wine is experiencing your own personal revival.

In the book of Job, the writer expresses the bursting feeling one has when filled with the wine of the spirit. He exclaims, *Behold, my belly is like wine that has no vent; the new wineskins ready to burst* (Job 32:19, ESV). You cannot be passive and without energy when you are filled with new wine. The Jewish philosopher Philo described this bursting with divine inspiration and energy as some form of "spiritual inebriation."[2]

Apostle Peter's sermon after the outpouring on the Day of Pentecost dispelled the accusations of drunkenness and explained the effect of new wine through the prophecy of Joel:

---

[2] NKJV Cultural Backgrounds Study Bible. Acts 2:13 note.

Men of Judea and all who dwell in Jerusalem, let this be known to you, and give ear to my words. For these people are not drunk, as you suppose, since it is only the third hour of the day. But this is what was uttered through the prophet Joel: "And in the last days it shall be, God declares, that I will pour out my Spirit on all flesh, and your sons and your daughters shall prophesy, and your young men shall see visions, and your old men shall dream dreams; even on my male servants and female servants in those days I will pour out my Spirit, and they shall prophesy." (Acts 2:14–18 ESV)

In addition to the effects of the new wine we have seen, the Joel prophecy shows that you will also be filled with prophecies, visions, dreams, and diverse encounters with the Holy Spirit. This is available to every single person. Not for Charismatics, Pentecostals, the young, or a particular type of people. He said, "*I will pour out my Spirit on all flesh.*" This includes you. Believe it and receive it. As you journey through this book, may you be filled with the new wine of the Lord!

The Restlessness of the Soul

*Hear my cry, O God,
listen to my prayer;
From the end of the earth I call
to you when my heart is faint.
Lead me to the rock that
is higher than I.*

—Psalm 61:1–2 (ESV)

There comes a time when you realize you are missing something on the inside. It could be a restlessness that will not shake off, a deeper need to seek the Lord in a manner different from the past, or a dissatisfaction with the status quo. You can make one of two decisions. The first is to consciously shake off the feeling and continue to do everything as normal. The second, which this book is about, is to decide to let go of the past and press into a new world. Moses, in the book of Exodus, came upon a tree that was burning. He had the same two choices: to keep moving along and ignore the tree or turn to the tree to investigate.

> *Moses was keeping the flock of his father-in-law Jethro, the priest of Midian; he led his flock beyond the wilderness, and came to Horeb, the mountain*

> *of God. There the angel of the LORD appeared to him in a flame of fire out of a bush; he looked, and the bush was blazing, yet it was not consumed. Then Moses said, "I must turn aside and look at this great sight, and see why the bush is not burned up." When the LORD saw that he had turned aside to see, God called to him out of the bush, "Moses, Moses!" And he said, "Here I am." Then he said, "Come no closer! Remove the sandals from your feet, for the place on which you are standing is holy ground."* (Exodus 3:1–5 NRSV)

When Moses turned to the tree, the Lord noticed his decision. He then called him by name, and this set a path of a revelatory encounter with God that changed the entire course of his life. A great change awaits you. What decision will you make?

The enemy of achieving greater things in our lives is living in past glory, traditions, or past methods that are working. Our justification is "don't rock the boat" or "if it ain't broken, don't fix it." In our journey with God, however, there is nothing like staying in the same place for a long time. God does not change; that is a given fact. However, it does not negate the fact that he is always moving. We may interpret the fact that he is on the move as he is changing. Even in a rapidly changing world, with changing standards, *his* standards have not changed. His attributes have not changed. His love for us and hatred for sin have not changed. Yet because he is moving, it seems as if he is changing, but he is not.

A perfect example of this is the prescribed manner of worship. God established a tabernacle of worship through Moses, which required people coming to God through a high priest, who would make sacrifices on behalf of the people in the tabernacle. This tabernacle was first erected in the deserts of Canaan. Over time, the tabernacle moved to Jerusalem, and everyone was required to travel to Jerusalem to worship. Within this period, there was a shift in God's communication with his people through the high priests to the prophets. Then God abolished the physical mode of worship through the tabernacle and sent his son, Jesus, into the world to be the ultimate sacrifice, bringing people into personal communion with him. He removed the priests and prophets from being mediators and established a simple way of coming to him through Jesus Christ, our perfect high priest. Once you accept God's new order through Christ, you have come to a place of personal worship and relationship with God. Through all these centuries of change, God himself never changed. His invitation and standard of entrance through worship is the same. The method is different. The exchange in the fourth chapter of John between Jesus and a Samaritan woman, who had begun to feel the restlessness initially referred to, summarizes the progression of God's interaction with man.

> *So he (Jesus) came to a town in Samaria called Sychar, near the plot of ground Jacob had given to his son Joseph. Jacob's well was there, and Jesus, tired as he was from the journey, sat down by the well. It was about noon.*
>
> *When a Samaritan woman came to draw water, Jesus said to her, "Will you give me a drink?" (His disciples had gone into the town to buy food.)*

DR. SUSAN AGBENOTO

The Samaritan woman said to him, "You are a Jew and I am a Samaritan woman. How can you ask me for a drink?" (For Jews do not associate with Samaritans.)

Jesus answered her, "If you knew the gift of God and who it is that asks you for a drink, you would have asked him and he would have given you living water."

"Sir," the woman said, "you have nothing to draw with and the well is deep. Where can you get this living water? Are you greater than our father Jacob, who gave us the well and drank from it himself, as did also his sons and his livestock?"

Jesus answered, "Everyone who drinks this water will be thirsty again, but whoever drinks the water I give them will never thirst. Indeed, the water I give them will become in them a spring of water welling up to eternal life."

The woman said to him, "Sir, give me this water so that I won't get thirsty and have to keep coming here to draw water."

He told her, "Go, call your husband and come back."

"I have no husband," she replied.

> *Jesus said to her, "You are right when you say you have no husband. The fact is, you have had five husbands, and the man you now have is not your husband. What you have just said is quite true."*
>
> *"Sir," the woman said, "I can see that you are a prophet. Our ancestors worshiped on this mountain, but you Jews claim that the place where we must worship is in Jerusalem."*
>
> *"Woman," Jesus replied, "believe me, a time is coming when you will worship the Father neither on this mountain nor in Jerusalem. You Samaritans worship what you do not know; we worship what we do know, for salvation is from the Jews. Yet a time is coming and has now come when the true worshipers will worship the Father in the Spirit and in truth, for they are the kind of worshipers the Father seeks. God is spirit, and his worshipers must worship in the Spirit and in truth."* (John 4:5–24 NIV)

The sign of her restlessness was the five husbands she had been married to, only to be with a sixth partner. You and I may not necessarily have been through five spouses, but our feelings of discontentment, which leads us to fill the void with "stuff" represent the different husbands we are going through. That's how one can graduate from beer to wine, to hard liquor, each time looking for a higher dosage of alcohol that will bring "joy" and a "high" that you can't find in the nondrinking life. How do you know that it's not real? The rate of descent from the fake happiness and the accompanying depression it leaves behind. Drugs can offer an alternative high, but with costlier medical consequences, including mental instability and ultimately death, after a series of overdoses. Video games, new relationships, fantasies, partying, and even vigorous participation in goodwill and charity are part of a long list of temporary pleasures the world offers to quench the emptiness that can overwhelm us.

When this Samaritan lady met Jesus, it was the end of her empty seeking. She had finally found what she had been looking for that she did not find in six different men. Today, when you meet Jesus, it is the same. He is the answer to the void, the emptiness, the restlessness found deep within. Her dialogue with Jesus is a great revelation for us all. She referred to the fact that her ancestors believed that worship should be on the mountain they were standing on; while the Jews insisted that worship should only be in Jerusalem where the tabernacle was. Jesus's answer was the beginning of a new way of coming to God because, once again, God was on the move. *"You will worship the Father neither on this mountain nor in Jerusalem."* Jesus was saying that worship will no longer be about a particular place. Then he goes on to say, *"We worship what we do know."* He takes away the notion of abstract idol worship of a "thing" and brings the lady into the reality that the God we worship is a real "person" whom you can know. Your worship should stem from the fact that you know Him. Jesus concluded with the statement: *"God is spirit, and his worshipers must worship in the Spirit and in truth."* Explaining that knowing God is about moving from a purely physical mentality to a spiritual one, because God is Spirit, and the spirit part of us must (a command) connect with him on a spiritual level through his Word, which is the truth. Symbols, traditions, and places of worship aid us in our corporate worship of God, but they are not a substitute for knowing him personally and walking with him.

Making the Leap

*But the Lord is the true God;
He is the living God and
the everlasting King.
At his wrath the earth quakes, and the
nations cannot endure his indignation.*

—Jeremiah 10:10

Whether you are currently a religious person, a nonreligious person, or a searcher of truths, you eventually become aware of a void within that needs to be filled. God made us that way. It is that internal discomfort that will drive us to him. Like the Samaritan lady at the well, once you find him, your entire world begins to change. Jesus is not an abstract idealistic icon conjured by religious fanatics. He is a real living and breathing being, the son of God sent from heaven to bring freedom from all manner of bondage to sin and to man. You have the free will and choice to either accept him or reject him. I encourage you to make the choice to accept him.

There are over ninety prophecies concerning Christ in the Old Testament that point to the fact that he is the Messiah that God was going to send. He stands today at the door of your heart and is knocking, and saying, "It is time." He is calling you to make a decision to believe. *Let me take your heavy burden, your frustrations, your emptiness, and let me give you life abundantly.* To make this leap of faith of letting go and stepping into Christ is a simple two-step process. First, believe and settle it forever in your heart that God is real. Believe that he sent his son, Jesus Christ, to save you from your bondage, from your past sins, and from eternal death. Second and last step, make this simple confession: "Dear Jesus, I am sorry for my sins. Please forgive me. I accept you as my Lord and Savior. I choose to believe in you and choose to follow you from today. Please write my name in the Book of Life. Amen." That's it. You are a new person, you are "born again," you are saved, and you are now part of the body of believers. Take your time to read these passages of scripture: 2 Corinthians 5:17–21, John 3:1–7, and John 3:16–17. You have just taken the most important step of your life!

After Taking the Leap

> *But the path of the righteous*
> *is like the light of dawn,*
> *Which shines brighter and*
> *brighter until full day.*
>
> —Proverbs 4:18

The decision to follow Jesus does not end with the confession. It is rather the beginning of a journey. Unlike natural journeys that have a beginning point and an end point, the journey in Christ ends wherever you choose to end it. You can end it at the confession, which means you never even began, a place many find themselves today. You can go a little further, seeking him in prayer, and end there. You can go even further by starting to dig into his truth (his Word) and end when you feel you know all that you need to know. The journey, however, as you can imagine, cannot have an end point because Jesus is not a finite being; and circling back to my introductory theme, God is always on the move.

> *But the path of the righteous is like the light of dawn, which shines brighter and brighter until full day.* (Proverbs 4:18 ESV)

NEW WINE

God is always on the move, and as you follow him, your path becomes more shiny or more glorious than it was before. This is your destiny—that you will move from one shining level to a more glorious one. Since he is always on the move, he causes a stirring on the inside of us that propels us to move in step with him. This is a different type of restlessness. Not the one that is accompanied by hopelessness, but one that is filled with anticipation of finding the treasure you are seeking. It is this stirring that will want you to move deeper into knowing God, and therefore worshipping him as he desires. The result is that your clarity of purpose increases, and your steps and your entire life become brighter and more hopeful. Knowing God is knowing his Word, which in itself has many depths of layers that the persistent will uncover. Knowing his Word is knowing Christ, who is *the word made flesh* (John 1:14). When God called Moses, one of the interesting conversations they had can be found in this text:

> *Then Moses said to God, "If I come to the people of Israel and say to them, 'The God of your fathers has sent me to you,' and they ask me, 'What is his name?' what shall I say to them?" God said to Moses, "I am who I am." And he said, "Say this to the people of Israel, 'I am has sent me to you.'"* (Exodus 3:13–14 ESV)

Moses, probably like you and me, wanted to know more about God. Who was he? How do you refer to him, how do you explain him? Imagine working for a company whose boss you have never met. And then you are sent to go and represent him or her at a conference. At that point, your chief aim is to gather as much knowledge as possible. Moses was in that boat. God was sending him to represent God himself to none other than the highest authority of the land, the pharaoh, and his enthusiasts. And Moses was at a loss because God was still mysterious, even though very real to him. God simply answered him, "Tell them 'I am' has sent you." *"Okay, that explains a lot,"* I'm sure would have been *my* response. Truthfully, it does explain a lot. It explains the fact that God is not limited to a word, a description, a time frame, a beginning, or anything. He simply exists. He simply is. It is a requirement you have to settle in your heart if you want to get anywhere with God. He is real, he is God, and he is like nothing we have ever seen or perceived or imagined. He is everything, and yet not limited to any one thing. And he wants you to know him.

Jesus, whom he sent, is also one with God. It is a mystery, yet a truth that transcends earthly logic. That is why Jesus told the Samaritan lady that a time was coming when it would not be about physical things but tuning in to a spiritual God. The earthly mind cannot figure it out. The spirit of a man, however, gets it and accepts it. The religious leaders of Jesus's day, steeped in earthly mind frames despite having memorized the scriptures, confronted Jesus often, not believing that he came from God. In one particular instance, they confronted him about his claims to be a Jew, priding themselves in their direct ancestry to Abraham, God's chosen patriarch.

> *Jesus answered, "If I glorify myself, my glory is nothing. It is my Father who glorifies me, he of whom you say, 'He is our God,' though you do not know him. But I know him; if I would say that I do not know him, I would be a liar like you.*

> *But I do know him and I keep his word. Your ancestor Abraham rejoiced that he would see my day; he saw it and was glad." Then the Jews said to him, "You are not yet fifty years old, and have you seen Abraham?" Jesus said to them, "Very truly, I tell you, before Abraham was, I am."* (John 8:54–58 NRSV)

After Jesus's response, *"Before Abraham was, I am,"* they picked up stones to stone him to death. No great surprise. Abraham lived many centuries before Jesus. The scribes and other religious leaders during Jesus's time had given themselves to study the scriptures. The scriptures then comprised the first thirty-nine books of the Bible authored by Moses, King David, and other major and minor prophets, known by the Jews as the Torah. They were well-versed in the promises of God to Abraham and his descendants and traced their heritage to Abraham. So when Jesus, who was in his thirties, and hadn't grown up in their religious circles talked to them about "Abraham rejoiced in my day" and "before Abraham I was," they were apoplectic in their feelings of outrage. They felt he was blaspheming. After all, which Torah school did he attend? Which synagogue had ordained him a scribe? Jesus was, however, revealing himself to them as the One sent by God, and if they had spiritual ears, would have heard the prophetic revelation in the name "I Am." They were waiting for the Messiah (and are still waiting by the way) and could not reconcile the Jesus who stood in front of them claiming spiritual heritage with Abraham, calling God his father, born in a lowly manger, with the Messiah they pictured would come and save them. Yet if they had ears, they would have heard the very words of God from the third chapter of Exodus saying, "Tell them I AM has sent you." *Before Abraham was, I AM.* The same words. Jesus is one with God. He was there at the beginning of creation. He is now seated at the right hand of God in heaven. Yet he is one with God. In pursuing God, Christ becomes the "door," as he says in John 10:1; and he is the "gate" of entrance into the things of God as we see in the elaborate pattern of the first tabernacle erected.

Jesus himself said, *I am the way, and the truth, and the life. No one comes to the Father except through me* (John 14:6 NRSV). Knowing God is knowing Christ, whom he sent. And knowing Christ is receiving revelation as he reveals himself through his Word. The next section is a brief compilation of Christ revealing himself through "I Am" sayings. Meditate on each "I Am" revelation and ask him to remove the veil, and open the eyes of your heart to encounter him!

Selah (Meditational Pause): I Am

I Am...The Bread of Life

Jesus said to them, "I am the bread of life. Whoever comes to me will never be hungry, and whoever believes in me will never be thirsty." (John 6:35)

* * *

I am the bread of life. (John 6:48)

* * *

I am the living bread that came down from heaven. Whoever eats of this bread will live forever; and the bread that I will give for the life of the world is my flesh. (John 6:51)

Jesus alone is the bread that satisfies the soul. If there is an unexplained emptiness, there is an opportunity to press into him to grant revelation as the bread of life, to fill that internal void. Lord, reveal yourself as the bread of life.

DR. SUSAN AGBENOTO

I Am...The Light of the World

"As long as I am in the world, I am the light of the world." (John 9:5)

* * *

Again Jesus spoke to them, saying, "I am the light of the world. Whoever follows me will never walk in darkness but will have the light of life." (John 8:12)

* * *

I have come as light into the world, so that everyone who believes in me should not remain in the darkness. (John 12:46)

Amid rising darkness around us, Jesus is light. He is the light that leads to the father, he is the light that brings hope to a spiraling world, and he is the light that alleviates one's personal darkness. Lord, reveal yourself as light in our lives.

I Am...Before Abraham Was

Jesus said to them, "Very truly, I tell you, before Abraham was, I am." (John 8:58)

Jesus is the eternal one. Though he walked the earth as a man for a span of time, he is in actuality without beginning and end. He operates outside of time, and for him, a thousand years can be as one day. May the Lord, the Eternal One, bring revelation regarding the mysteries of eternity and cause time to work in our favor.

I Am...The Door

I am the door. If anyone enters by me, he will be saved and will go in and out and find pasture. (John 10:9)

* * *

So Jesus again said to them, "Truly, truly, I say to you, I am the door of the sheep." (John 10:7)

Jesus is the door to new realms in the spiritual journey. He is the door to the pasture that nourishes us and prospers us. Where there may be ambiguity on which next steps to take or which door to open, there is an opportunity to press in for the revelation of Christ who is the keeper of the doors of life.

I Am...The Good Shepherd

I am the good shepherd. The good shepherd lays down his life for the sheep. (John 10:11)

When King David referred to the Lord as his shepherd in the twenty-third Psalm, he specified the characteristics of a good shepherd. In the care of the good shepherd, there is no lack. He restores the soul, he brings guidance, and he delivers from the machinations of the enemy. May you experience this and more as the Lord Jesus reveals himself as the good shepherd in your life.

I Am...The Son of God

Can you say that the one whom the Father has sanctified and sent into the world is blaspheming because I said, "I am God's Son"? (John 10:36)

The mystery of the Godhead is that God is God the Father, God the Son, and God the Spirit. Jesus is the Son of God. During his time on earth as a man, he taught many things and spoke many words that are still life-giving today to those who believe. When he died, he took the reproach of our sinful nature, granting the promise of eternal life. May you experience the power of God flowing in and through your life as Jesus reveals himself as the son of God.

I Am...The Resurrection and the Life

Jesus said to her, "I am the resurrection and the life. Those who believe in me, even though they die, will live." (John 11:25)

Where God is, there is life. He transferred authority to us when he said death and life are in the power of the tongue. In situations where the spirit of death hovers, where there is decay, may there be an infusion of life as Jesus reveals himself as the resurrection and the life!

I Am...The Way, The Truth, and The Life

Jesus said to him, "I am the way, and the truth, and the life. No one comes to the Father except through me." (John 14:6)

To know God is to know Jesus Christ, his son, whom he sent. May he reveal himself to you in greater measure, and may your eyes be open to truths you need for your life!

I Am...The True Vine

I am the true vine, and my Father is the vinegrower. (John 15:1)

* * *

I am the vine, you are the branches. Those who abide in me and I in them bear much fruit, because apart from me you can do nothing. (John 15:5)

We are the branches of the eternal vine. Without the sap flowing from the vine to the branches, there is no fruitfulness. Where there is barrenness, frustration, and even desperation, there is an opportunity to press into the one who is the vine. May you experience new life flowing through you as you connect with and receive revelation of the true vine!

Pressing Into Him

*The law and the prophets
were until John.
Since that time the kingdom of
God has been preached
And everyone is pressing into it.*

—Luke 16:16 (NKJV)

Once again, in this relationship journey with Christ, you are the one who determines the end point. You go as deep as you are willing to go. There is always more. There are times when the Lord himself will prompt you to prepare to go deeper into the waters, and there are times when *you* have to take the initiative. There are even times you will find yourself plunged into it unprepared and possibly unwilling. You cannot let your past or your present dictate where you are going. You were created to go from one shining destination to a shinier one (remember Proverbs 4:18). When your past has shades of glory in it, it is much more difficult to press into a higher place because the sense of achievement blocks that desire.

    To press into a deeper place comes with a desperate desire and a willingness to lay down the old things. To lay down the old way of doing things. Perhaps you have always prayed a certain way, at a certain time, with a certain style. Perhaps even with the same scriptures. Or perhaps you have never experienced communion with the Lord through prayer and worship. God is calling you to go deeper. He is inviting you to cultivate closer communion with his Holy Spirit. Perhaps your knowledge of Christ is what you learned in Sunday School or snippets of a pastor who remembers to talk about Christ's attributes when he is preaching. God is calling you into deeper revelatory knowledge. Perhaps you have never heard God speak to you, never sensed the Holy Spirit leading you, and have never tangibly encountered Christ. It is time for a new beginning in your life. And it begins when you willingly lay down your trophies, your achievements, your defenses, even your failures, doubts, and traditions and come before him in total surrender. Lay it all down and cry out to him in total desperation, "I surrender, and I desire a closer walk with you, Lord Jesus."

Let's look at another conversation Jesus had with a group of religious leaders who didn't like the fact that Jesus's disciples were not fasting as they should.

> *They said to him, "John's disciples often fast and pray, and so do the disciples of the Pharisees, but yours go on eating and drinking."*
>
> *Jesus answered, "Can you make the friends of the bridegroom fast while he is with them? But the time will come when the bridegroom will be taken from them; in those days they will fast."*
>
> *He told them this parable: "No one tears a piece out of a new garment to patch an old one. Otherwise, they will*

have torn the new garment, and the patch from the new will not match the old. And no one pours new wine into old wineskins. Otherwise, the new wine will burst the skins; the wine will run out and the wineskins will be ruined. No, new wine must be poured into new wineskins. And no one after drinking old wine wants the new, for they say, 'The old is better.'" (Luke 5:33–39 NIV)

This conversation with Jesus revolved around fasting. The religious leaders once again had an issue. According to their deep studies and devotion, if Jesus was truly who he said he was, he and his disciples should be adhering to the traditions of fasting. They could not imagine that this person whom they did not see fasting was claiming any kind of calling. As a side note, fasting was not commanded in the Mosaic law except for the fast on the annual Day of Atonement, but the scribes and Pharisees had adopted fasting as part of their rigorous lifestyle. Jesus, on the other hand, was found at banquets, weddings, and all manner of events, presumable feasting. Jesus's response was neither to reject nor systematize fasting but rather drew attention to the need to be sensitive to the timing of a fast. Using himself as a symbol of a bridegroom, he asked them if one could fast as a bridegroom, or even a friend of a bridegroom during a wedding season? In the Jewish culture, it is offensive to fast or to not partake in the activities during a wedding you have been invited to, probably because of the connotation of mourning that fasting has. Jesus was using it to explain that he, the eternal bridegroom, had been manifested on earth; and as a result, it was not a season of mourning, but of rejoicing. He went on to note that the season was not a long one because the bridegroom would soon be taken away, and then the seasons of fasting could continue.

The Lord could be calling you into a new season of prayer, of fasting, of waiting on him which is different from what you have been doing. He will lead you by his Holy Spirit. Resist the urge to continue in your traditional way of doing things like these Pharisees and allow the Holy Spirit to lead you into your season of "new wine." Jesus himself fasted privately, as we see in his forty-day fast in the fourth chapter of Matthew. He also taught how to fast in an unannounced fashion (Matthew 6:16) and even rebuked the disciples at one time that they could not cast out a demon tormenting a boy because *this kind goeth not out but by prayer and fasting* Matthew 17:21 (KJV). God has not changed his mind about the need to fast nor has the power released through fasting diminished. God is, however, emphasizing relationship with him, so he alone should know about your fast, and he promises that he will reward your secret fasting life openly.

After this discourse in fasting, Jesus gives this interesting proverb. First, he says, *"No one tears a piece out of a new garment to patch an old one. Otherwise, they will have torn the new garment, and the patch from the new will not match the old."* With the discussion of fasting in mind, the "new garment" is all the great blessings and new moves of God through Christ, and the "old garment" is our traditions and old mindsets. Jesus is clear about one thing here: the two do not mix, and even will stymie the move of God if this cohabitation is forced. If you want to be in step with a God who is on the move, you have to shed the past mindsets. Don't be surprised if you find that your perspective on different things begins to change, which could be an indication of the new direction the Lord may be leading you to. Jesus goes on to give a second example: "*And no one pours new wine into old wineskins. Otherwise, the new wine will burst the skins; the wine will run out and the wineskins will be ruined. No, new wine must be poured into new wineskins.*"

In ancient times according to various studies, wineskins were made of goatskins and used to hold wine. The liquid was poured into the goatskin while it was in the fermentation phase of freshly crushed grape juice. As the fermentation took place, the wine would expand in volume, causing the goatskin to stretch. If the wineskin was new, it would stretch as the wine fermented and increased in volume. But if the wineskin was a used one, already stretched, it would break because there was no more room for expansion as the wine volume increased during fermentation.

It becomes necessary to lay aside what you have known, to relax the rigidity of attained knowledge and what you believe to be "the way," and allow the Lord through his Spirit to lead you into a greater place, different from what you may have known. It may be time for your skein to be stretched beyond comfort, beyond your acceptable ways, but it is worth the discomfort, far more than you will ever know.

Wine of Revival

*So they were all amazed
and perplexed,
Saying to one another "Whatever
could this mean?"
Others mocking said, "They
are full of new wine."*

—Acts 2:12–13 (NKJV)

Jesus wants to pour into us the new wine of revival fire, fresh power, healing, a new anointing, and a new kind of beauty because God is, once again, on the move. The hindrance to this outpouring of new wine is our old wineskins. We are afraid of letting go of what we have known and trusted in.

The first time I encountered someone laughing uncontrollably in a service, I was uncomfortable and wanted it to stop. Then it happened to me, and I couldn't control the joy and laughter. The Holy Spirit was pouring out the oil of joy, and the manifestation could be in so many different ways. Old wine says, *it's not of God, stop it*. New wine allows the wine to flow. There are indeed many fake manifestations, exaggerations, and pure darkness posing as light in the midst of the new, but we do not need to throw out the baby with the water. I've seen people vibrating under the power of God, I've seen oil appearing on the hands of saints during an assembly, I've been knocked down as hands were laid on me and God did a new work in me. I once had a personal retreat in Pensacola, Florida, after I had heard it was the location of the Brownsville revival. I tangibly experienced the Lord's presence and was blown away by one of the worship services I attended on a campus nearby. It felt as if the room was crowded with angels who had joined in the worship because the sound was unearthly, and the feeling was as I had never felt before.

    The fourth chapter of Revelations explains that the angels live in a state of worship, and as they worship, everyone else (I will add, both in heaven and on earth) joins in. So when you find yourself in a worship setting, know that there are angels who are immediately drawn to you because you are doing the very thing they love to do. The things of the spirit are real, and as the last days approach, sensitivity to the things of the spirit will be integral to people believing the gospel.

    The new wine of the Lord leads to both personal and corporate revival. The Day of Pentecost could be categorized as one of the first corporate revivals since the resurrection of Christ. There have since been many corporate revivals. One such revival, known as Azusa Street, was the place of the outpouring of the spirit that ushered the generation into speaking in tongues again coupled with other signs and wonders as stewarded by William Seymour. Another is the Toronto Blessing under the stewardship of John and Carol Arnott. Then the Brownsville revival, the Welsh revival, and many other revival fires that have since been lit all around the world. The next chapter will look at some of these revivals briefly in chronological order. I echo Katherine Kuhlman's sentiment when she is quoted saying, "I believe in miracles, because I believe in God." Revivals are significant because they involve masses of people being touched and stirred into relationship with God by the power of the Holy Spirit. They don't come in any pattern or form and can even offend the traditional minister. Yet they have been instruments of mass conversions and tangible displays of the power of God. These power displays of God are a clarion call for his people to come back to him.

I remember attending a vineyard church program in Boston. The pastor was recounting the testimony of a season when they had been praying for the rain of revival, and one day in the middle of the service, it started to rain in the sanctuary while it was dry outside! God will reveal himself in different ways as you seek him. James 4:8 assures us of this: *"Draw near to him, and he will draw near to you."* As you pursue God, not necessarily the miracles, but God himself, he will truly reveal himself to you in so many different ways. You just need to be open to recognize and receive it.

There have been different seasons when I have been led to physically go to my church to pray for long hours. I have done that as a church member, and I have done so as a pastor. Each time, it has been the initiation into a new season of my life spiritually speaking. In one of those seasons, I would pray from about 5:00 p.m. when I closed from work till about 9:00 p.m. at church. One particular day as I prayed, my phone was not off and rang. In surprise, I looked at the caller and realized it was the overseer over our region calling, and I answered the phone. He was sending me on an assignment to another state. As I spoke with him about this assignment, I walked toward the exit of the church toward my car to grab my charger since my battery was running low. When I opened the door, a few meters ahead of me stood a huge being with his arms crossed, just staring at me. I stepped to the left, where I had parked my car in front of the church building, and saw one of the kids from church walking in my direction. By the time I turned back to this being, he was gone. And this was all in the space of less than a few seconds. I asked the kid if he saw the person standing there, which would have been right in his path, and he said he never saw anything and went on to say he deliberately scouted his surroundings whenever he walked. I understood that the being was an angel, and his presence served as a confirmation to me of the assignment I was being given in that season. Get ready to be shifted out of your comfort zone!

The Wine of Revival Flows through Men

> *Then those who gladly received
> his word were baptized;
> And that day about three thousand
> souls were added to them.*
>
> —Acts 2:41 (NKJV)

There is much said about South American revivals stewarded by Claudio Freidzon, pastor of Rey de Reyes (King of Kings) Church. His church seats about twenty-five thousand people on a Sunday. Thousands would gather in a stadium for a service he would advertise, and when they were asked who Freidzon was, they had no clue but were just hungry for God and came. God used him mightily, but the glory ultimately belonged to God. It was the work of the Holy Spirit to gather the people in masses at the mention of Freidzon without knowing who he was. He was the vessel that God had chosen for some of these South American revivals. Through the vessel, many are touched and empowered to go and reach others.

Out of one of his meetings, a seven-year-old girl sitting in her classroom in Argentina began to pray, and as her teacher rebuked her, she called for the Holy Spirit, and thump, there went her teacher on the ground, knocked down by the power of God. Her classmates followed their teacher on the ground, shouting for Jesus as they lay on the ground. Yes, that's revival, and somewhere deep in our spirits is a longing for that stirring of the Creator. Let us look at some revivals that different parts of the world have experienced.

The Second Great Awakening (1730s–1740s)

This was a revival that impacted the English colonies in America when religion was losing a foothold because of the philosophical movement known as the Enlightenment.[3] Jonathan Edwards, an Anglican minister, and George Whitefield, a missionary to America, together with slaves, and native Americans were instrumental in this revival. The movement was characterized by a wave of "emotional preaching and fervent, enthusiastic worship."[4] Thousands of new converts came to the faith, and there was a renewed faith in God.

The Second Great Awakening (1800s)

About fifty years after the First Great Awakening ended, another one began in the New England area marked by another renewal of interest in religion. During this revival, churches had explosive growth, and denominations such as the Methodists and Baptists grew rapidly. Many colleges and seminaries were also birthed in this movement.

---

[3] "The First Great Awakening," History, retrieved September 17, 2023, https://www.history.com/topics/european-history/great-awakening#section_2

[4] Duke Taber, "List of Revivals in History: How God has Transformed the World," retrieved September 17, 2023, https://viralbeliever.com/list-of-revivals-in-history-223.

The Welsh Revival Great Awakening (1904–1905)

The Welsh revival broke out in Wales in 1904. Roughly one hundred thousand people were converted during the course of the revival, which spread without any advertisements or promotions. Evan Roberts was one of the principal agents used by God in this revival. Roberts had been praying daily for thirteen years and had had some dynamic encounters with the Lord including four-hour trances. This revival trickled into other countries, birthing many churches abroad with a focus on evangelism and missions.

The Azusa Street Revival (1906–1915)

On April 9, 1906, William J. Seymour, an African American preacher, and some men were praying when similar to the Day of Pentecost, they felt something like a bolt of lightning hit them and knocked them onto the ground. They began to speak in other tongues, shouting and praising God. Crowds gathered as this phenomenon lingered and news of it spread. People found themselves slain by the spirit as they approached the gathering. Many were baptized in the spirit, and there were countless testimonies of healing. This revival was significant because it incubated interracial and intercultural worship and was a major catalyst in the birthing of Pentecostalism.

The Healing Revivals (1940s–1950s)

This era of the 1940s and 1950s was packed with many men and women of God who carried a mantle of revival in the United States. At the same time in East Africa, there was a similar revival taking place that started in Rwanda and spread to parts of the Congo, Uganda, and Kenya.[5] The East African revival helped shape the Anglican Church at that time. In the States, William Branham, with his miraculous healing campaigns, had begun a wave of mass gatherings characterized by signs and wonders, healings, and other notable miracles. He is acknowledged by most to be the "father" of revivals in this era. There is a black-and-white photo captured from one of his meetings where there was fire falling on the masses gathered, their hands lifted in prayer and worship. A few years later, Oral Roberts came on the scene, also mantled with a healing ministry, gathering masses, with myriads of healing and salvation testimonies. Other well-known names through which the healing movement lingered were Jack Coe, A. A. Allen, and many other prominent servants of God.

The Toronto Blessing (1994)

The Toronto Airport Vineyard church was pastored by John and Carol Arnott, who were greatly inspired by revivals happening in South Africa and then in Argentina, stewarded by Claudio Freidzon. They had been praying for revival in their church and were led to invite Randy Clark, a Vineyard Church pastor, and associate of Freidzon. Randy was scheduled to minister January 20–23, 1994. The series of meetings ended up going twelve and a half years with services every day except on Mondays. Randy Clark preached those first sixty days, and the attendance the first year went from about one hundred people to one thousand. Characteristics of the services included laughing, roll-

---

[5] Kevin Ward, *The East African Revival: History and Legacies* (Surrey, England: Ashgate Publishing).

ing, and being slain in the spirit. The focus of this revival, which has lingered and birthed other revivals such as the Brownsville revival, and Holy Trinity Brampton church (England) among many others, was experiencing deep levels of God's love. Every year, thousands of people still flock to Toronto to experience what is still ongoing and known as the Toronto Blessing. The church name changed from Toronto Airport Vineyard to Catch the Fire Toronto.

The Brownsville Revival (1990s)

The Brownsville Assembly of God in Pensacola, Florida, began on Father's Day, June 18, 1995. Like the Arnotts in Toronto, Pastor John Kilpatrick had been leading the church to pray for revival. He invited Steve Hill, who had been impacted by the Toronto Blessing through the Holy Trinity Brampton church, as a guest speaker. On one of the nights, it is reported that there was a sudden "mighty wind" that came into the sanctuary and threw him down, lifted the pulpit, and swung it to the back of the church. The people were immediately hit by the power of God, knocked down to their knees, calling out in repentance to God, and sobbing in total surrender. This lasted for months and, eventually, a couple of years. Hill's speaking engagement was extended, and he preached several nights over the next five years. Between 1995 and 2000, more than four million[6] people are believed to have attended one of the Brownsville services from all around the world.

---

[6] "Fire From Above," *Charisma Magazine* (June 2005).

DR. SUSAN AGBENOTO

The Asbury Revival (2023)

The Asbury revival in more recent times was sparked when students at the Asbury University in Wilmore, Kentucky, tarried in prayer after a regular Wednesday service. On February 8, 2023, spontaneous worship and prayer followed the scheduled service with the students refusing to leave the hall, prompting the president to send out an email: "There's worship happening in Hughes. You're welcome to join."[7] Asbury had experienced a similar revival in 1970 that heavily influenced Methodism and the Jesus Movement. This time, however, with the use of social media, students posted what was happening on their personal social media accounts and attendance to the services grew up to fifteen thousand people a day. It is hard to categorize the meetings as "services" since the students just stayed in the auditorium night and day, worshipping and praying. This revival was unique in two aspects. It's accidental stewards were of the Gen Z generation and prioritized fellow Gen Z attendees' participation in the revival. At one point, the entrance into the building was closed to persons above the age of twenty-six since the focus of the revival was the youth reclaiming their faith in Christ. The second unique aspect of the revival was that on February 24, 2023, the university made a decision to shut down the revival, noting the reason being "the Asbury team was just fried, and there was decision fatigue, and just burnout."[8] The school

---

[7] Monica Kast, "As Asbury revival winds down, participants say experience 'redirected our priorities,'" *Lexington Herald Leader*, retrieved February 27, 2023.

[8] Fiona Morgan, "The Asbury Revival is Over. What Happens Now?" https://ministrywatch.com/the-asbury-revival-is-over-what-happens-now/#:~:text="The Asbury team was just fried, and there, hope is that revival continues in other spaces.

believed that its role was complete and hoped that those who participated would take the revival back to where they came from. Over fifty thousand people were reported to have visited from around the States and beyond in those two weeks.

In Conclusion

This very brief and not at all exhaustive outline is to give perspective on how real and how vast the move of God is. These events are also mentioned to wake up something dormant on the inside and to stir up an appetite to reach out beyond the bounds of the ordinary. Finally, it is a call to pray for corporate revival in your church and in your region. We need new wine poured upon our cities and our congregations today. Become a spiritual steward of your church and your city, praying and declaring as the Lord Jesus taught us, *Lord, let your kingdom come!*

The framework of this book was birthed in a meeting in 2018 hosted by Heidi Baker, who was impacted by the Toronto Blessing. I remember being amazed sitting in that meeting as Claudio Freidzon of the South American Revivals spoke of revival and evangelism. It began a new season of awakening within my spirit. As you read this book, you are partaking in that supernatural atmosphere, and I pray the Lord brings you into a new season of encounter with him and that your spirit is provoked to go into greater depths in him as you have never known. Weeks after that meeting, I was in one of our church services during worship when the eyes of one of the worshipers were opened to see an angel on my left and another on my right, both holding swords as they paced. I understood it to be the sign of a new era. May you find yourself moving into a new era of your spiritual walk in Jesus's name!

DR. SUSAN AGBENOTO

Much as the supernatural has framed my view of the Christian journey, I recognize that God is *still* on the move and is doing more things, even greater things, and things that are very different from what I have seen and heard of. One such shift is toward the evangelistic focus. It seems as if there is a fresh mantle of crowd gathering to simply hear the message of pure salvation. Billy Graham was a leading evangelistic voice in the mid to latter 1900s as well as Reinhard Bonke. Another such vessel being used mightily is the Bishop and Evangelist Dag Heward-Mills. He holds Healing Jesus Campaigns in different African countries and hundreds of thousands of people gather to hear the beautiful message of Christ's saving power. The preaching is regularly followed by miraculous healings and miracles. Todd Bentley was also being used in a similar fashion in Lakeland, Florida, and Randy Clark as well in the Central and Southern American regions. Pastor Jerry Eze has between fifty thousand and one hundred thousand people praying with him on the Internet from all over the world from 7:00 a.m. to 8:00 a.m. Nigerian time every Monday through Friday. This is not discounting the many different revival fires that are being lit all around the world by many servants of God in this season. God is on the move!

Let It Go

*Beloved, I do not consider that
I have made it my own;
but this one thing I do:
forgetting what lies behind
And straining forward to
what lies ahead,
I press on toward the goal for
the prize of the heavenly call
of God in Christ Jesus.*

—Philippians 3:13–14 (NRSV)

If God has moved in a certain way in the past, it is not a guarantee that he will do so in the future. It becomes imperative for us to let go of our past to embrace the new. It takes a certain level of trust in God to let go of what you know in order to embrace the future. You can hold on to your past experiences, but in doing so, it may cost you discerning God's new leading for your life.

Then they said to him, "John's disciples, like the disciples of the Pharisees, frequently fast and pray, but your disciples eat and drink." Jesus said to them, "You cannot make wedding guests fast while the bridegroom is with them, can you? The days will come when the bridegroom will be taken away from them, and then they will fast in those days." Luke 5:33–35 (NRSV)

"The days will come," Jesus says, signifying the essence of seasons. He was saying that there was a season for fasting. Don't "camp" where you are or where you have been. A still river is a dead one, and eventually collects algae, developing a stink. Churches and ministries that camp in one season of God's move become a still river and die off. There may still be members, worship, and so on, but spiritually it's dead because they did not move on with the one who said, "Out of your belly shall *flow* rivers of living water." He said "flow" not "stay." We tend to stay because it is our comfort zone, or even more dangerous, it has been our past formula for success. We always sing three songs of praise before the Word. We always start with prayer. Sister Gloria must by all means sing her solo, which signifies the spirit "coming." The word *orthodox* has become a "no bueno" word in charismatic circles because it signifies a certain rigidity that the charismatic claims to have shaken off. The word *charismatic* has a similar effect in the Orthodox world because Charismatics are perceived to be all spirit with no depth of theology.

Gradually, however, the Charismatics have also begun to camp at the "shaking off the orthodox" and developing their own set ways. Camped at staying in the church to have more services instead of going out to reach the lost. Camped at becoming very interested in titles and comparing ministries instead of serving. This is not a criticism of any denomination but rather a highlighting of Jesus's words when he said, *"The days will come."* There are seasons to everything, and we have to be in constant pursuit of the God who is on the move, forcing ourselves out of habitual encampment, being ready to let go of our reputation, our comfort, and our natural tendencies in order to be in step with him.

Perhaps you have known a certain type of worship in your life or a certain way of religion or have even related with certain people in a way that needs to change because the seasons have changed. When I met my first-ever roommate, she was simply Diana. Diana the prayer warrior. Diana who could be in the room for a whole day just crying out to the Lord to anoint her. Diana my roommate. Then God called her to lead the music ministry in our church, and she became my leader, and the seasons of relating with her simply as roommate and friend changed. Then God called her to pastor a church. The seasons yet changed again. We were no longer roommates, or even in the same state, but we kept in touch as close friends; however, she was now Pastor Diana, and I treated her as such.

You can "flow" with the change and march on to your blessings, or you can resist it because you are afraid of what it might entail, or you may be too proud to find yourself going into what you may think to be a lower place. God has promised that if we will humble ourselves, he alone will lift us up (James 4:10). I will paraphrase that verse to say, "Don't resist the season of being a seed in the soil, God will make sure your season of breaking forth will come." As you try to lift yourself in a season that you must lay low, you will find that you will be high for a short-lived time and fall back to the ground speedily, simply because God resists the proud (James 4:6). Be sensitive to, and live in obedience to what God is doing. Don't fight your soil time. Don't hang on to what is already dead. Let it go!

Your Time Down in the Soil

*Truly, truly, I say to you, unless a grain
of wheat falls into the earth and dies,
It remains alone; but if it
dies, it bears much fruit.*

—John 12:24

Nature acquaints us with the seasons of life when we need to be proverbially buried underground and fully covered to grow. The making of wine starts its journey at the level of the grape seed. The seed's time in the soil is crucial to its destiny. A plant's soil time is its time to germinate so that it may grow into that beautiful plant, shrub, or tree. Similarly, a caterpillar starts life pretty small and has a phase where it's ensconced in a cocoon, unseen and unheard until such a time when it blossoms into a butterfly. For each one of us, there is that phase where we are covered, unseen, unheard, down in a place that seems almost dark. It's a necessary phase because, without it, a certain type of growth, beauty, and even fruitfulness does not happen in our lives. The most poignant example nature gives us of being buried is the embryo in the womb. For nine months, the human life starts in minuscule form in a womb in an enclosed sac. This sac contains the nutrients the embryo needs for its formation until its birth nine months later. If the embryo decides it has had enough of being covered and wants to come out before the appointed time, it will not have life for very long. Returning to the example of the seed, here is an excerpt from Penn State's College of Agricultural Sciences:

> When a dry seed comes into contact with moist soil or growing media, the seed begins to take up water through the seed coat. As it takes up more water, the seed expands and the seed coat cracks open. The embryo inside the seed is made up of a small shoot and a small root. The root is the first to emerge from the seed. As it grows, it anchors the plant to the ground, and begins absorbing water through the root. After the root absorbs water, the shoot begins to emerge from the seed.[9]

There is a seed season we go through where we are covered, buried, not seen, not heard, and not even seeing or hearing much ourselves. Like a plant's seed, the season in the soil gives us the necessary nutrients to strengthen us for life's phases ahead. James 1:2 talks about counting it all joy in this season and letting patience work its perfect work in us. We cannot rush the season, but we can intentionally develop patience. In such seasons, you wait. As you wait, the nutrients from patience strengthen you until your proverbial seed coat expands and cracks open, birthing from within a root that eventually anchors the plant to the ground.

---

[9] "Understanding Seeds and Seedling Biology," College of Agricultural Sciences, retrieved September 20, 2022, https://extension.psu.edu/understanding-seeds-and-seedling-biology.

The mightiest of trees are anchored by the sturdiest of roots, and the roots take years to form. Have you thought to yourself, "There is nothing happening in my life," or "I'm in such a dark place, I feel invisible"? Allow time to cultivate the precious gift of patience in you.

> *My brothers and sisters, whenever you face trials of any kind, consider it nothing but joy, because you know that the testing of your faith produces endurance; and let endurance have its full effect, so that you may be mature and complete, lacking in nothing. (James 1:2–4 NRSV)*

Some other versions use the word *steadfastness* rather than *patience*. When you think about the verse from the standpoint of the formation of roots for a mighty tree, steadfastness brings the point home. Through the seasons of rain, and snow, and storms, and even heat, the roots patiently form underground. Your time in the soil is an opportunity to become strong in many aspects of your life. This is where emotional strength is built as well as spiritual, mental, and even physical strength in the form of stamina. You will need that strength because the next phase of growth will involve the growth of branches and eventually fruit, which your roots will have to be strong enough to carry.

Many successful actors, musicians, athletes, and even religious ministers who do not spend enough time in the soil end up disintegrating when they start to bear the fruit of success. The pride alone crushes the roots, and as they bear fruit for the public to see, their internal system slowly collapses. The next step is to turn to something that can carry them: drugs, alcohol, inappropriate relationships, and so on. In some cases, it even leads to their death. I address this soul brokenness in the book *Restore Me!*[10] It is the same phenomenon of the child who is not disciplined growing up. The absence of restraint and boundaries is exacerbated in adulthood, bringing a similar collapse if there is no intervention. The soil time is crucial for all of us. The soil time kills enemies such as pride, self-righteousness, entitlement, and greed, which are brought on by the fruit we eventually bear.

How do we develop this patience and steadfastness? In one word, *surrender!* There isn't anywhere to go anyway, so you might as well intentionally channel that phase into a place of willing surrender to God. That involves you resisting the thoughts from hell that you are worthless. It is easy to receive and accept thoughts that you are done, you are irrelevant, you are worthless when you are in that going-nowhere-soil season of your life. But God does not waste opportunities and seasons, he is working in you and on you even then. Your job is to resist the devil's suggestions of worthlessness and despair. Perhaps you have been looking outward for validation. Looking to family, to friends, to coworkers to validate who you are. It's time to start looking upward to the Lord instead, which is a component of intentional surrender to him. First, you have to be convinced of his love for you. If he did not love you or want you, he would not have created you to begin with. You are chosen. Affirm yourself.

> *I praise you, for I am fearfully and wonderfully made. Wonderful are your works; that I know very well.* (Psalm 139:14 NRSV)

---

[10] Dr. Susan Agbenoto, "*Restore Me! But Privately Please.*" Westbow Press, 2024.

Your surrender also means you start praying into the next season of your life. Your prayers must not only be prayers of *faith* but infused with *hope*. You will make it. You will come out. You are in seed time, but after that, harvest time will come. Remember when Jesus said the Kingdom of God is like a mustard seed...He said this seed *is the smallest of all the seeds on earth, yet when it is sown it grows up and becomes larger than all the garden plants and puts out large branches, so that the birds of the air can make nests in its shade* (Mark 4:30–32 ESV). Remember as you pray that the Lord will turn your ashes into beauty. He will turn your barrenness into fruitfulness. Have faith in God. Know that it is well. He wants you to know his heart: *I know the plans I have for you, they are plans of good. I will not stretch you beyond your threshold of what you can handle* (Jeremiah 29:11, 1 Corinthians 10:13). May the Lord reveal himself to you as you wait in patience and willing surrender!

Make New Wine of Me

> *Therefore thus says the*
> *LORD, the God of hosts:*
> *Because they have spoken this word,*
> *I am now making my words*
> *in your mouth a fire,*
> *And this people wood, and*
> *the fire shall devour them.*
>
> *—Jeremiah 5:14*

You see, the expression "on fire" is a literal feeling of fire that you can experience. It's not just an expression for someone who can quote four scriptures and attends prayer meetings. You can do that and have no fire burning inside of you. Our continuous prayer to the Lord should be "Keep me burning for you, let your new wine pour forth into me continuously." You can be so much in love with the Lord of Glory, so full of his Spirit, that you feel like something inside of you is going to burst as eloquently expressed in Job 32:19.

    In the twenty-fourth chapter of the book of Luke, after Jesus had risen from the dead, he appeared to two of his disciples and began to speak with them. Initially, they did not recognize him, but Christ the Word revealed himself to them through the explaining of many spiritual concepts. As he spoke, they gradually became enlightened until they recognized him, at which point Christ vanished from their sight. The result of their encounter with Christ is reflected in their conversation afterward: *They said to each other, 'Did not our hearts burn within us while he talked to us on the road, while he opened to us the Scriptures?'* (Luke 24:32 ESV). They actually felt a burning, a fire blazing inside of them as they had their encounter with the Lord. The process of new wine flowing through us is the process that activates fresh fire to burn within us. This is the place where it seems something fuels you to either shout, jump, or sit up! A literal fire sizzles through your spirit, and when it does, by all means, cry out to the Lord for more of him as you find yourself in that place.

The common theme that runs through men and women who have been used for the spectacular, who have had this fire burning within them, is a certain level of hunger for God. I continually pray that as you read this, your spirit will catch fire, inspiring you to call out to God to wreck you completely for him. Hunger for the Lord will drive you to him and cause him to come near to you.

> *Draw near to God, and he will draw near to you. Cleanse your hands, you sinners, and purify your hearts, you double-minded.* (James 4:8)

As you draw near to God in hunger, he will draw near to you in a more tangible way. He will meet you at the point of your hunger. It is a hunger that holds no conditions. There is no "Lord, I will do anything except..." or "Lord, you can do whatever, except for my kids..." Neither is there a bargaining of your time, "Lord, as I sacrifice my time to seek your face and pray, give me..." There is a time for supplication, a time for intercession, and a time of simply hungering and thirsting for the Lord himself. Waiting on the Lord as a result of your hunger for him is not about what he can do for you, but rather a simple desire to just be with him. The psalmist in the forty-second Psalm cries out poignantly:

> *My soul thirsts for God, for the living God. When can I go and meet with God?* (Psalm 42:2 NIV)

He wanted to just meet with God. Sometimes, it is as simple as asking God that you want to meet with him and be with him. It is so simple that we bypass it and go onto what we have deemed more spiritual pursuits. I remember once being in a meeting with a man of God after a season of fasting and praying. He was praying for various people, and because of the time of praying and fasting I had gone through, I was expecting a rather glorious prayer over my life. His exhortation for me, however, was that he believed the Lord was saying to me that I wasn't spending time with him as I used to. I felt like the "good" man Jesus spoke of who had followed all the commandments but was sad to hear he had to sell all his property to be near to the kingdom. He did not know that he was following hard after the commandments to cover up for his deficiency in the love of money. Coming close to Jesus reveals our most hidden cover-ups, and he lovingly gives us the grace to let go so that we might inherit all the things ordained for us. I had been fasting and praying, which are "good" but not in itself the ultimate in seeking the face of God. The psalmist said:

> *When you said, "Seek my face," My heart said to you, "Your face, Lord, I will seek."* (Psalm 27:8 NKJV)

Waiting on God goes beyond prayer. It is coming to a place of total surrender as you abandon everything to just be with him. It could be in silence, meditation, listening, worshipping, or praying in the spirit for long hours. And the position of your heart in those times is "Lord, in your time, I am listening, and in your leading, I will obey; whatever." No conditions, no agenda, just a simple longing to be with his being. The attitude, like the psalmist, is simply *"Your face, Lord, I will seek."* In that place of intimacy, he pours *new wine* upon us, and fruitfulness is born. You in him, and him in you, with no distractions, time pressures, or self-willed motives. The Lord was saying to me, I appreciate your prayers and fasting as you have been taught because they reflect your devotion to me and my work, but it has caused you to not just sit with me. It was a hard lesson, but effective in learning the difference between the two.

After the psalmist responds in the twenty-seventh Psalm, he goes on to pray: *"Teach me thy way, O Lord, and lead me in a plain path, because of mine enemies."* The psalmist in this eleventh verse is asking the Lord to teach him and lead him. Being in his presence reveals our lack of knowledge and propels us to seek his guidance. I am encouraged by the part of the prayer that says *"lead me in a plain path,"* which indicates that the paths of the Lord are not always plain, and even King David, a lover of God encountered those instances when God's leading was not plain. This caused him to ask the Lord to lead him in a plain manner where he would not miss what God was saying or directing.

May God teach you his ways and lead you in a plain path as you pursue Him. May the Holy Spirit help you navigate the new paths chartered ahead for you. May you experience the fire of burning in your heart, and may he fill you with *new wine!*

The Science of Crafting New Wine

*Neither is new wine put
into old wineskins;
Otherwise, the skins burst,
and the wine is spilled, and
the skins are destroyed;
But new wine is put into fresh
wineskins, and so both are preserved.*

—Matthew 9:17 (NRSV)

When we are crying out to the Lord for *new wine*, what are we really asking? Let us take a look at the science of wine making in the natural. Wine making can be generally classified into five stages: harvesting, crushing and pressing, fermentation, clarification, and finally aging and bottling. Winemakers unanimously agree that good wine begins with good fruit. It is the prelude to the success of the first stage: harvesting. The planting, grafting, and caring for the seed crop produce a harvest of grapes worthy of great-tasting wine. In Isaiah chapter 5, God refers to us as his choice vines that he has planted and hedged. He is the farmer or the husbandman watching over us, his vineyard, and because he created us as choice vines, he expects good fruit to come out of us. He expects great-tasting wine to flow from us. We need to be concerned when the fruit coming out from us is not in line with what the Word of God has prophesied about us.

Harvesting, Crushing, and Pressing

The first stage of harvesting is the stage in which the grapes are carefully plucked. Once the grapes are harvested, they are sorted and undergo crushing and pressing for the juice, called *"must"* to be extracted. The must at this stage is a raw joule with skins (if it's red wine), seeds, and solids in it. In the making of white wine, the skins are immediately extracted in order not to color the wine. This stage is an apt description of the process we go through in preparation for the season of new wine. The season of new wine could entail experiencing the miraculous and being used by God in an extraordinary manner. It is a season of being pressed, inconvenienced, suffocated, persecuted, and even being hidden. It will long precede your emanating the power, the fragrance, and the new wine of God. Everyone has their unique journey, and unique time and type of pressing, just as we see even in the differences in the treatment of white versus red wine. Your hunger for the Lord, in those times, is what would keep you seeking him and trusting him through the crushing. And God is looking for that heart that can withstand the fire and still turn to him. Being used by God comes with an unfortunate deception that the greatness comes from you because of something you are doing right. The fire of the trials presses that pride out of you as you stand in the limelight.

Fermentation

Once the juice is extracted, it is now ready for fermentation. This is where yeast (either natural or added) converts all the sugar in the *must* into ethanol (alcohol). This is a one-to-two-week process. If the winemaker wants the wine to remain sweet, he cuts short the period of fermentation so that some of the sugar is preserved. The unique aspect of fermentation is that there is no actual process, it's just a matter of waiting. As you press into asking God for more, to move beyond the status quo, you will encounter this fermentation stage of "waiting." In Psalm 27:8, we recall the Psalmist saying, *"When you said, 'Seek my face,' My heart said to you, 'Your face, Lord, I will seek.'"* Then later on in verse 14 adds, *"Wait for the LORD; be strong and take heart and wait for the LORD."* He was exhorting us to come before God with no agenda, no time pressures, just waiting on him to speak, to lead, to guide, and to move.

The fastest way to move God is to wait. On him. A cycle is usually birthed where we come to know God intimately through seasons of waiting on him, which ushers us into ministry because of the resulting weight of his presence and anointing upon us. In the busyness of ministry, however, the waiting slowly recedes, reducing the level of the anointing, until we dry up, and the very ministry we love becomes an albatross we can no longer effectively carry. God points out in Jeremiah 10:21 that not waiting on him as a minister will result in you not prospering personally and your flock scattering. It is a serious verse to pay attention to as a minister of God. Fermentation for us must happen frequently, allowing the sugar "stresses" to evaporate as we wait on him so that we can receive that pure and power-filled new wine.

DR. SUSAN AGBENOTO

Clarification

After fermentation is the stage of *clarification*. Here the solids are filtered from the fermented *must* and transferred into a different container. It's a time of separation. Waiting on God naturally results in separation from what is usually a distraction in your life. It could be separation from toxic friends, certain types of entertainment, idle activities, and other things that have filled our days and lives. You will have to learn how to be sensitive enough to the Spirit of God to know that today is not movie night, it's "spend time in his presence" night. He will never force you nor will he condemn you if you disobey him because his love for us throughout our journey never wanes. Your obedience and sensitivity, on the other hand, will cause him to draw nearer and pour more of himself into you. Have you ever been around someone who carries the weight of his glory? I remember being in a conference, sitting close to the front with my eyes closed in worship and prayer when I felt the presence of the servant of God walk in from the back of the sanctuary. He had that heavy a presence. When you examine their lives, they seem almost restricted in their ways. That very voluntary restrictive life is what has also produced the glory they carry. Everything has a price. Even the anointing. If you want to watch movies every night and allow just about anything into your spirit, there is nothing that prevents you from doing that, and God thoroughly enjoys you anyway. Do not be surprised, however, if you walk in the lowest level of anointing that was ordained for you. Everything has a price. As much as God loved his only son, God paid the price of watching his beloved son die a terrible, tragic, senseless death on a filthy cross in order to enjoy the benefit of saving a world he created in love. Even God paid a price.

NEW WINE

Aging and Bottling

The final stage in wine making is allowing the wine to age and eventually be bottled. This fine wine is now put in containers after some more aging or, in layman's terms, more time elapses. Different corks or bottle tops are chosen to close the bottles according to the taste the winemaker is going for. Two passages quite significant to this process are found in the first and second books of Corinthians. The first is:

> *There are diversities of gifts, but the same Spirit. There are differences of ministries, but the same Lord. And there are diversities of activities, but it is the same God who works all in all. But the manifestation of the Spirit is given to each one for the profit of all.* (1 Corinthians 12:4–7 NKJV)

The new wine is from the Lord but is administered differently in different vessels or bottles. The choice of cork or top for the bottle explains that "the manifestation of the Spirit is given to every man," but "there are differences of ministries." I can have the anointing and power of Aimee McPherson without having to be exactly like Aimee McPherson. I can press in for her anointing, but ultimately it is God who will do that transfer, and when it is manifest, I will still not be called Aimee McPherson. God chose your "bottle" type as well as your "cork" type according to the unique administration of the wine He has given you.

The second scripture is:

> *But we have this treasure in earthen vessels, that the excellence of the*

power may be of God and not of us. (2 Corinthians 4:7 NKJV)

God has ordained this new wine in us, his chosen earthly vessels so that we will show off the power of his glory. It's entirely about God and not us. And it is one of the reasons why such power and anointing will flow through totally flawed human beings like us so that there is no mistaking what the source of the power is. Our lives were created to bring him glory. As you go through these different phases, hang on to the promise that at the end of the challenges and dark times is greatness as he pours new wine into you.

Walking the Road

Then he said to them all,
"If any want to become my followers,
let them deny themselves
And take up their cross daily
And follow me."

—Luke 9:23 (NRSV)

Are you ready to walk on the road called "new ground" road? It looks a little different for everyone. For Joseph, he needed to get off the *old ground road* of his brothers who didn't believe in his calling or giftings, and the path was seventeen years of imprisonment for something he didn't do. Yet he never wavered in his faith and total yielding to God. He came out straight from prison to be granted rulership delegated by the ruling pharaoh. For Moses, his *old ground road* was the environment of the king's palace where he lived as a prince but not received as the one to deliver his fellow Israelites from bondage. God allowed him to transition from the palace to hard desert life for forty years. When that was complete, he brought him into the role of being Israel's first shepherd, bringing them out of the darkness of Egypt. Daniel was taken away from his home, exiled to Babylon, and made a eunuch without choice. In the end, he was known as a man of great wisdom and "light," and he reigned as prime minister spanning three different kings.

Your passage may not have entailed spending forty years in the deserts of Morocco, nor being imprisoned unfairly, nor being exiled into another country. God, however, has a custom-designed road to bring you into the place of new ground. There is something about the comfort of our homes and traditions that keep us from aligning ourselves with the new thing God is doing. It is necessary to evacuate from the old grounds, and at times, it takes some real shaking in our lives to uproot us. He will at times create these new ground road experiences to wake us up, shake us up, and stir us up until we can hear his voice and hear his heart and follow him. If you are experiencing a senseless shaking, you may be a prime candidate for being ushered into a new season! In your journey, you will notice a recurring theme of Christ calling you to himself. A call to know him on a more personal note, to be more sensitive to his nuances, a stirring of a deep thirst on the inside for more. Choosing this book and reading it is part of your stirring into a new season. Before this book was published, I prayed for you many times. I believe your season is changing! Perhaps your validation and spiritual confirmations have always come from men, but in this new season, God says, "I am your validation. I am your confirmation. Trust me."

> *When he has brought out all his own, he goes ahead of them, and the sheep follow him because they know his voice. (John 10:4 NRSV)*

Not only does he want you to look to him for validation, he wants you to know his voice. Knowing his voice is an important attribute to develop as you go along this journey. Going back to the story of Moses, we see that at the kairos moment, God revealed himself to Moses through a bush that was burning but did not burn (Exodus 3:1–5). It was the beginning of quite an extraordinary relationship between God and Moses. Of course, God had already marked Moses from the foundations of the world to be in relationship with him by simply bringing him into the world. That moment of the bush burning was Moses's eye-opening to an eternity-long truth—the truth that the God who created the universe exists, loved him, and was waiting for him to come into that revelation, to result in relationship with him. It's the same with you. God created you because he loves you and spent a long time planning exactly how you would be like, what you would be called, and your unique destiny on earth as you align yourself with him in relationship. You are not a mistake. And as dysfunctional as you may think your family is, your placement there was not a mistake either. Once Moses made the connection, his life changed significantly with manifestations of signs and wonders not entirely replicated today. The key was being away from familiar grounds and coming to know the voice of his shepherd intimately.

Many times we develop the art of pleasing our religious leaders to the point where we substitute their voices for God's voice in our lives. God's voice must be real in our lives to the point where we are able to hear God speaking when they speak, distinguishing the divine from the temporal. Without knowing God's voice, every voice you hear seems significant to you, and you find yourself running hard in a direction not meant for you, sweating profusely but achieving little. May you know him. May you know his voice. May you know his leading and guidance. This will lead you into a more glorious destiny. May that be your portion in Jesus's name!

Breaking Point

*The sacrifices of God
are a broken spirit;
A broken and contrite heart, O
God, you will not despise.*

—Psalm 51:17 (ESV)

The journey to your more glorious destiny will involve the word *breaking*. The psalmist refers to a "broken spirit" and a "broken heart" in the fifty-first Psalm. This is important to hear if you are going through an extremely difficult time. Instead of the enemy using that as permission to flood you with spirits of depression and heaviness, it can rather be a season of great visitation from the Lord as he finds our spirits more open in those times. Without knowing it, we accumulate junk in our spirits as time goes by. Our hearts become cluttered with bitterness, disillusion, offense, cynicism, and pride amidst all sorts of silent diseases that make our hearts and spirits so full that they create a veil between us and God. Usually, we don't realize that this process is taking place until God starts to reveal it to us. The cluttered heart makes us less yielding to him and less open to correction because we believe we are already correct. We are then less likely to follow in a radically new direction because we have the guardrails of self-righteous spiritual caution up all around us.

To break through all that junk, God has to start the process of heating the environment until, like metal, we reach the temperature called the melting or breaking point. Here, we can be remolded into what the Savior has originally intended for us. This season of increased heat and melting is critical for all who go through it because if you don't yield and the molding starts, you simply break. These are seasons where it seems the ground has been taken from under you. I remember once going through a season of intense disappointment and initially starting to go into warfare, binding the one who comes to steal, kill, and destroy.[11] Not long into that resolve, the Lord revealed to me that it was him at work. I had to learn to go from fighting in the spirit as I was accustomed to, to yielding to the potter.

What does yielding look like when your very being is boiling in the hot waters of adversity, disappointment, and mindless hurt? It starts with trust. Trust that the Lord who created you and formed you with such a deliberate process is at work in your life and cares about you. Trust is what helps you to let go and say, "I yield to your careful hand." Trust also says, "Though it makes no sense, I believe you are at work, so I will endure it." There will always be options to fight, to defend yourself, to stop the season of hardship. The result is a delayed manifestation and even a repeat of that season since you did not complete the course. Yes, it takes discernment to decipher whether you should surrender to the Lord or bind the enemy trying to destroy you, and I pray that you will receive discernment concerning your journey. The eighth chapter of Romans assures us

---
[11] John 10:10

that "*all things work together for good to them that love God.*"[12] Yielding starts with trust, followed by leaning toward his Word rather than your constant analysis of what could have been.

> *Trust in the Lord with all thine heart; and lean not unto thine own understanding.* (Proverbs 3:5)

We desire that everything we go through makes sense to us. God does not promise us that. He rather says, "*For my thoughts are not your thoughts, neither are your ways my ways,*"[13] so we should expect that things will not always make sense to us. The natural mind in times of distress seeks to escape, wants revenge, and wants justice, but "*leaning not on your understanding*" means you forfeit the right to all those things.

There will be well-meaning voices that will coax you to revert to seemingly logical reasoning that will encourage revenge and that will remind you that you've been cheated enough! Your trust must end in a resolve that categorizes these voices in a firm place called "well-meaning but not destiny." Listening to those voices weakens your trust as the building of trust involves a complex interplay of the heart as well as the mind. The mind has to lean decisively toward the Lord and his promises and not on the natural analysis of its circumstances. Doubt must be eradicated with purposeful strength.

When Peter the disciple was beckoned to walk on water, his heart was already in the place of trust, which dared him to take the first step. His mind on the other hand, had not. It had yet to come into full agreement

---

[12] Romans 8:28
[13] Isaiah 55:8

with his trusting heart. This was because his mind was processing a raging storm, contending with his heart's simplistic trust. He took the first few steps boldly as his heart led him, but as the natural sounds and sights began to rage harder, his mind could not keep up with the calm of his heart. I can only imagine waves bigger than him threatening to swallow him whole, the very ocean he was walking on rising and ebbing as if he was surfing, thundering noises of crashing waters threateningly set against a backdrop of darkness. Is that not what our dark seasons look like? Issues trying to swallow you up, the familiar ground you have walked on removed from under you as things change for the worse rather rapidly, as the voices around you stimulate doubt, fear, and hopelessness. It may have seemed as if Jesus had left him for a moment. It may seem as if God *has* left you for a season. Jesus, however, never left; he was always there. And when Peter reached the drowning point at which he felt it was too much for him, he cried out to Jesus who *immediately* stretched out his hands to rescue him.

> *But when he saw that the wind was boisterous, he was afraid; and beginning to sink he cried out, saying, "Lord, save me!" And immediately Jesus stretched out His hand and caught him, and said to him, "O you of little faith, why did you doubt?"* (Matthew 14:30–31)

Jesus is there immediately to save us so that we don't drown, a fact that should guarantee our trust. It becomes necessary to intentionally turn our minds onto the promises of God and rehearse them until it is strong enough to drown the voices of doubt, revenge, and hopelessness that tend to assault us in seasons of trials. The breaking point is not set to destroy us, but to prepare us for more glorious seasons ahead. Anchor yourself in his promises and don't give up until you see the light of your path shining brighter and brighter!

A New Beginning

*And he said to him,
"Every man at the beginning
sets out the good wine,
And when the guests have
well drunk, then the inferior.
You have kept the good
wine until now!"*

—John 2:10 (NKJV)

In the second chapter of John, there was a wedding in the city of Cana that had the unfortunate issue of running out of wine. This would bring huge embarrassment to the hosting family. You may have been in a place in your life where you felt like you had run out of wine. You may have run out of joy in the Lord, out of energy, and don't see much of anything changing in the future. Jesus's mother, the wise woman of the hour, turned to her son and told him plainly, *They have no wine* (John 2:3 ESV). Throughout this book, there has been a gentle invitation to similarly turn to Jesus. Mary followed this up with an instruction to the servants, *"Do whatever he tells you."*

This writing may have given you a fresh perspective on some of the things you are going through or what kind of season you are in. It may also have given you perspective on the bigger picture of what the Lord is doing beyond your sphere of awareness. Even yet, you may have received understanding concerning the fact that your purpose is not finished and that there are greater things ahead. In all your insights, hold this counsel close to your heart, *"Do whatever he tells you."* This is the path to having the best wine.

First, Jesus said, *"Fill the jars with water."* This was an instruction that made no sense. If they wanted to serve water, they would not need intervention. Some of the instructions of the Lord may not make sense to us. The disciples had toiled all night, and Jesus came into the boat and told them to cast the net, again, as if they had not been doing so all night. Yet when they obeyed, *at his word*, they brought in a harvest as they had never seen. Obedience to the little things, as well as the seemingly big things, results in success.

Jesus's next words were *"Now draw some out and take it to the master of the feast."* He did not make any declarations or manifest any extraordinary display. He just said that the "water" be drawn out and taken to the master. When the Lord is doing something in our lives, we subconsciously expect it to be accompanied with elaborate signs. This is not always the case. When Elijah had his encounter with God, the scriptures painstakingly make a note of this:

> *He said, "Go out and stand on the mountain before the LORD, for the LORD is about to pass by." Now there was a great wind, so strong that it was splitting mountains and breaking rocks in pieces before the LORD, but the LORD was not in the wind; and after the wind an earthquake, but the LORD was not in the earthquake; and after*

the earthquake a fire, but the LORD was not in the fire; and after the fire a sound of sheer silence. (1 Kings 19:11–12 NRSV)

Elijah was probably expecting something wild, like the wind breaking rocks and God emerging from above or God displaying his power through the earthquake, but God was in neither. Most translations say God came to him afterward in a "still small voice." The NRSV is even more dramatic in describing the aftereffect as "sheer silence." God can be moving, but all you sense and hear is *sheer* silence. That does not mean the Lord is not at work. Trust in God and his promises despite what you see or don't see. When the servants at the wedding drew out the liquid, one can only imagine their amazement when they saw that the color of the liquid had changed!

When the wine was presented to the host, he called the bridegroom and said to him, *"Everyone brings out the choice wine first and then the cheaper wine after the guests have had too much to drink; but you have saved the best till now."* Better years are ahead of you. As you make time to hear him, obey him, and trust him, it will be said of you, this is the best we have seen of him or her yet. The wine pouring out of you will be better, sweeter, and more powerful. The prophecy, as we see in the book of Proverbs is that your path will shine brighter and brighter (Proverbs 4:18)!

May you experience a new season in which you overflow with new wine, with fresh fire, with rekindled desire for the Lord. As this chapter closes, may you receive an impartation from heaven above as you open your heart to receive more of Christ. There *is* more. Go after the "more" in the Lord. Get up from your place of camping. Wake up from your sleep. Seek his face. Listen for his voice. Engage with the Holy Spirit who is your eternal guide. May you be molded into a vessel of revival, a vessel of his kingdom. May you experience the power of God, and the manifestation of his gifts as you have never imagined. May your devotional life be transformed as you are led by his Holy Spirit.

The next and final chapter consists of prayers that I have prayed over you many times before this book was published. I prayed that you would experience the intimacy, the hunger, the supernatural, and the awesome presence of the living God. I encourage you to pray along these prayers, open the scripture references as well, and declare them back unto the Lord.[14] The appendix contains some resources that could be a stepping stone to experiencing even greater impartation. God bless you!

---

[14] Isaiah 43:26

Prayers

Let us pray together:

- I pray over you fresh fire, a fresh anointing, and fresh power!
    - Matthew 3:11

- I pray over you a deep hunger for God and for all things God!
    - John 7:37–38

- I pray over you that you will experience revival in your spirit, revival in your soul… kingdom revival!
    - Matthew 6:10

- I pray over you that you will stand, no matter the wind that blows, no matter the rain that pours, the test or trial, that you will stand.
    - Ephesians 6:13

- I pray over you that you will experience a spiritual breakthrough, a breaking through walls, through obstacles, through resistance, through the status quo.
    - Psalm 18:29

- I pray over you that you will come into violent desperation in the Lord that will manifest in unique spiritual encounters with him.
  - Matthew 11:12

- I pray that you will have a life-changing visitation of the Lord.
  - Revelation 4:1

- I pray over you that you will receive a touch of heaven.
  - Revelation 4:1

- I pray over you that every bondage over you will be broken in Jesus's name!
  - Isaiah 10:27

- I pray that in every area that you are experiencing barrenness, emptiness, or restlessness, the Lord will begin to fill you with more of him!
  - Matthew 5:6

- I pray over you that the heavens will be open over you, and you will breakout...breakout...breakout!
  - Isaiah 66:1

- I pray that every negative experience you've had, and every scarring of your soul will be healed as you move into a new phase of your journey.
  - Psalm 23:3

- I pray that you will be liberated from chains that bind and destroy and that you experience life and freedom in Christ!
  - John 8:36

NEW WINE

- I pray over you that you will be molded into a vessel of new wine!
  - 2 Timothy 2:22

- I pray over you that you will experience the burning of the heart as the word of God finds root within you.
  - Luke 24:32

- I pray over you that every sin you are struggling with that has become a stumbling block, you would be delivered in Jesus's name!
  - Hebrews 12:1–2

- I pray over you that you will not be distracted by the issues of this world, but you will develop eyes and focus for the Lord alone.
  - Colossians 3:1–2

- I pray over you that you will know experientially the love of Jesus, which surpasses all knowledge and understanding.
  - Ephesians 3:19

- I pray over you that where you have experienced deep loss and sorrow and are even still in mourning, the Lord will bind your broken heart and grant you to laugh again.
  - Isaiah 61:1

I Want To Hear From You

The best part about writing this book was the times of prayer and promptings of the Holy Spirit. I prayed for you many times. I would like to hear from you. Whether it's just a comment, a question, or a desire to pursue a subject I simply touched on, reach out. If you even want to set up an appointment for someone to pray with, reach out. Susan.agbenoto@gmail.com.

Resources

Here are some recommended readings:

- The Bible (any version)
- Any good devotional book that will aid you in your reading of the word of God
- *The Great Azusa Street Revival*, compiled by Roberts Liardon
- *Christian Beliefs* by Wayne Grudem
- *Foundational Truths for Christian Living* by Derek Prince
- *The God Chasers* by Tommy Tenney
- *God's Generals* by Roberts Liardon
- *God Runner* by Will Hart
- *I Believe in Visions* by Kenneth Hagen
- *Intimacy with God* by Randy Clark
- *Sweet Influence of the Anointing* by Dag Heward-Mills
- *Truth Therapy* by Dr. Pete Bellini
- *Fire on the Prayer Altar* by Dr. Susan Agbenoto (pending release)
- *Restore Me, But Privately Please*, Dr. Susan Agbenoto (pending release)

Bibliography

Agbenoto, Susan. "Restore Me! But Privately Please." Westbow Press, 2024.

College of Agricultural Sciences. "Understanding Seeds and Seedling Biology." Retrieved September 20, 2022. https://extension.psu.edu/understanding-seeds-and-seedling-biology.

History. "First Great Awakening." Retrieved September 17, 2023. https://www.history.com/topics/european-history/great-awakening#section_2.

Charisma Magazine. "Fire From Above." June 2005.

Kast, Monica. "As Asbury revival winds down, participants say experience 'redirected our priorities.'" *Lexington Herald Leader*. Retrieved February 27, 2023. https://www.kentucky.com/news/local/education/article272537740.html.

Keener, Craig S., and John H. Walton. NJKV Cultural Backgrounds Study Bible. Zondervan, 2017.

Morgan, Fiona. "The Asbury Revival is Over. What Happens Now?" Retrieved September 17, 2023. https://ministrywatch.com/the-asbury-revival-is-over-what-happens-now/#:~:text="The Asbury team was just fried, and there, hope is that revival continues in other spaces.

Taber, Duke. "List of Revivals in History: How God has Transformed the World." Retrieved September 17, 2023. https://viralbeliever.com/list-of-revivals-in-history-223.

Ward, Kevin. *The East African Revival: History and Legacies*. Surrey, England: Ashgate Publishing.

About the Author

Meet Dr. Susan Agbenoto, who will navigate your perspectives into those beyond the physical, and will inspire you to boldly identify and grasp spiritual concepts you can practically apply. Susan obtained her Doctor of Ministry degree from The United Theological Seminary, and has been serving as a lay pastor within a large church network.

Though she works with an Investment company and analyzes figures to articulate their embedded story, she still finds time to immerse herself in reading and fine-tuning various literary pieces and half-jokingly declares that "there is always more to write, but a book must have an end." Apart from writing, Dr. Agbenoto has been invited to speak in both religious and corporate forums. Outside of her writing adventures, Dr. Agbenoto likes to travel and experience the authenticity of other places, especially places with rich ecclesiastical narratives.

Her curiosity, faith, and love for God and his Word, immerses you into a place of restorative hope and renewal. Her conversational tone while explaining practical spiritual concepts make her books easy to read. Dr. Agbenoto's intertwining passions of prayer and the study of theology, translates into a tangible encounter with the divine as you read, leaving you intellectually stimulated, spiritually refreshed and wanting more.

Milton Keynes UK
Ingram Content Group UK Ltd.
UKHW030627280824
447491UK00001B/80